AF438640

THE ART OF RESILIENCE

THE ART OF RESILIENCE

Thriving in Today's World

B. VINCENT

QuillQuest Publishers

CONTENTS

Copyright © 2024 by B. Vincent

All rights reserved. No part of this book may be reproduced in any manner whatsoever without written permission except in the case of brief quotations embodied in critical articles and reviews.

First Printing, 2024

Introduction to Resilience

Grasping Versatility

Versatility is frequently compared to the strength and adaptability of bamboo, which twists under the power of a tempest yet seldom breaks. In human terms, strength is the mental and profound courage that permits people to bounce back from difficulty, injury, misfortune, dangers, or critical wellsprings of stress. It's not just about persevering through difficulty; it's tied in with adjusting, developing, and arising more grounded from difficulties.

At its center, flexibility includes an intricate interchange of considerations, activities, and ways of behaving that anybody can create and fortify. This part will demystify the idea of versatility, showing that it's anything but a natural quality moved by just a lucky few however a bunch of abilities and perspectives that can be developed and sustained in anybody.

Significance In this day and age

In the present quick moving, continually impacting world, the capacity to be strong is more important than any time in recent memory. Worldwide occasions, individual disturbances, and the everyday stressors of current life can test our soundness and inner serenity. From managing the vulnerabilities of a worldwide pandemic to exploring the intricacies of individual connections and work difficulties, versatility goes about as a cushion, empowering us to confront and beat these obstructions.

This segment will investigate the different spaces of life where strength is vital, featuring stories and models that show its worth. We will address the most recent exploration that features how strength adds to in general prosperity, emotional well-being, and achievement. The objective is to furnish perusers with a reasonable comprehension of why creating strength isn't simply gainful yet fundamental in this day and age.

Outline of the Book

This book is organized to direct the peruser through the different components of flexibility, from understanding its establishment and the way that it tends to be sustained inside oneself, to its application in private connections and expert conditions, and its importance in the more extensive local area and social settings.

We will investigate the mental underpinnings of versatility, offer functional exhortation and activities to assemble flexibility, and offer moving accounts of people and networks that have shown surprising strength despite difficulty. Every section is intended to give significant bits of knowledge and noteworthy systems, making the specialty of versatility open to everybody.

•Part 1: The Underpinnings of Flexibility plunges into the fundamental credits that comprise versatility, like mindfulness, the ability to appreciate people on a deeper level, and good faith.

•Part 2: Individual Flexibility centers around how people can develop internal strength and versatility.

•Section 3: Relational Versatility looks at the job of connections in building and supporting flexibility.

•Part 4: Proficient Versatility takes a gander at strength in the work environment and how to flourish in the midst of expert difficulties.

•Section 5: Social and Local area Strength extends the idea to bigger cultural and social structures, underscoring aggregate flexibility.

•Section 6: Instruments and Procedures offers down to earth direction for creating flexibility, including activities and propensities to cultivate a versatile outlook.

•Part 7: Looking Forward thinks about the eventual fate of strength, tending to arising difficulties and how flexibility can be an instrument for development and development.

Our process together will be one of revelation, learning, and strengthening. Toward the finish of this book, perusers won't just comprehend what flexibility is nevertheless will have the devices and information to assemble and outfit their own strength and flourish in this day and age.

Chapter 1: The Foundations of Resilience

In this part, we dive into the bedrock of flexibility, revealing the fundamental credits that structure its establishment. These characteristics, including mindfulness, the capacity to understand people on a profound level, and positive thinking, are intrinsic qualities as well as abilities that can be created and upgraded after some time. Understanding and developing these qualities are vital stages toward building versatility, engaging people to explore life's difficulties with elegance and strength.

Mindfulness

Mindfulness is the cognizant information on one's personality, sentiments, thought processes, and wants. It's the foundation of versatility, empowering people to perceive their responses to stress and affliction. By creating mindfulness, one can distinguish individual triggers, grasp profound reactions, and start to oversee responses in a solid, helpful way.

Key Parts of Mindfulness:

•Profound Acknowledgment: Understanding one's personal state is the most important move toward mindfulness. It includes perceiving feelings as they happen and recognizing them without judgment.

•Self-Evaluation: Consistently thinking about one's assets, shortcomings, and standards of conduct. This reflection helps in recognizing regions for development and advancement.

•Care: Rehearsing care upgrades mindfulness. It includes remaining present and completely captivating with the second without interruption or judgment.

The ability to appreciate individuals at their core

The capacity to appreciate people on a deeper level (EI) is the capacity to comprehend and deal with one's own feelings, as well as perceive and impact the feelings of others. It's a significant component of versatility, as it works with exploring complex social scenes, keeping up with positive connections, and pursuing smart choices under tension.

Four Mainstays of The capacity to understand individuals on a deeper level:

•Self-Administration: The capacity to control imprudent sentiments and ways of behaving, deal with feelings in sound ways, and adjust to evolving conditions.

•Mindfulness: As recently talked about, remembering one's feelings and their effect.

•Social Mindfulness: Grasping the feelings, needs, and worries of others, and getting on close to home prompts.

•Relationship The executives: Creating and keeping up with great connections, imparting obviously, moving and impacting others, functioning admirably in a group, and overseeing struggle.

Idealism

Idealism, a confident point of view, is a principal part of versatility. It's not necessary to focus on overlooking life's difficulties yet rather keeping an uplifting outlook towards the future, even despite misfortune. Positive thinkers will quite often see deterrents as impermanent and accept they have command over their future, empowering them to continue in their endeavors and recuperate from mishaps all the more rapidly.

Developing Good faith:

•Reevaluating Negative Considerations: Changing a negative outlook into a positive one through mental rebuilding, zeroing in on potential arrangements as opposed to issues.

•Appreciation Practice: Routinely recognizing and valuing what's great in life can move center based on what's missing to what's plentiful, cultivating positive thinking.

•Future-Situated Thinking: Defining objectives and picturing a positive future can persuade activity and support a confident viewpoint.

Coordinating the Establishments into Day to day existence

Understanding and fostering these primary ascribes are the most important moves toward flexibility. In any case, the critical lies in coordinating and rehearsing these abilities in day to day existence. This includes cognizant exertion, for example,

•Keeping a diary to improve mindfulness and the capacity to understand people on a deeper level.

•Rehearsing care through contemplation, profound breathing, or different strategies.

•Taking on an appreciation propensity, for example, recording three things you're grateful for every day.

•Testing negative contemplations and zeroing in on certain results.

As we expand on these establishments, strength turns out to be something other than an idea — it turns into a lived insight, a piece of our regular routines. This section has laid the foundation for the excursion ahead, where we will investigate how to apply these standards to encourage self-improvement, reinforce connections, and flourish in the expert world.

Chapter 2: Personal Resilience: Building Your Inner Strength

This part investigates the core of flexibility: the individual excursion toward developing internal strength and versatility. Building individual strength is tied in with fostering the psychological, close to home, and mental determination to explore life's high points and low points. It includes upgrading our ability to deal with misfortune directly, adjust to change, and arise not just solid however more grounded and more fit. Here, we dig into techniques and practices that cultivate individual flexibility, guaranteeing people are ready to address difficulties with certainty and beauty.

Embracing Affliction as Any open door

The most vital phase in building individual strength is to reevaluate our point of view on difficulty. Rather than review difficulties as inconceivable obstructions, versatile people consider them to be amazing chances to learn, develop, and fortify their determination.

Procedures for Embracing Affliction:

•Development Outlook: Developing a development mentality, which embraces moves as opportunities to extend one's capacities and information.

•Affliction Remainder: Fostering a misfortune remainder, or AQ, which estimates one's capacity to manage difficulties. It's tied in with expanding one's capacity to bear distress and vulnerability.

•Intelligent Practice: Routinely pondering past difficulties and the systems used to beat them. This reflection can give bits of knowledge and lift trust in dealing with future troubles.

Creating Close to home Spryness

Profound deftness is the capacity to explore one's feelings with care and adaptability. It permits people to answer life's progressions and difficulties without being overpowered by pessimistic feelings.

Key Parts of Close to home Spryness:

•Distinguishing Close to home Examples: Perceiving repeating profound reactions and grasping their triggers.

•Venturing Out: Making a psychological space among feeling and activity, considering more intentional and less receptive reactions.

•Strolling Your Why: Adjusting activities to basic beliefs, even notwithstanding difficulties, which gives a directing compass during fierce times.

Building Mental Sturdiness

Mental sturdiness alludes to the mental edge that empowers people to stay engaged and steady under tension. It's tied in with having the certainty and inspiration to continue on toward an objective, in spite of misfortune.

Parts of Mental Durability:

•Certainty: Confidence in one's capacities, which energizes perseverance and exertion.

•Control: Feeling in charge of one's life and fate, as opposed to helpless before outside occasions.

•Responsibility: A firmly established assurance to accomplish objectives, no matter what the impediments.

•Challenge: Review difficulties as any open doors instead of dangers, which cultivates flexibility and development.

Cultivating an Emotionally supportive network

Nobody fabricates strength in detachment. A solid emotionally supportive network assumes a basic part in creating individual versatility. It gives a wellbeing net of close to home and commonsense help, support, and exhortation.

Developing Strong Connections:

•Looking for Associations: Effectively constructing and sustaining associations with family, companions, coaches, and friends who offer help and understanding.

•Local area Commitment: Partaking in gatherings or networks with shared interests or difficulties can offer a feeling of having a place and common help.

•Requesting Help: Perceiving when to look for help and being available to getting support from others.

Reasonable Strides for Reinforcing Individual Versatility

•Put forth Practical Objectives: Spotlight on feasible objectives to cultivate a pride and progress.

•Practice Self-Empathy: Indulge yourself with graciousness and understanding, particularly during difficult stretches.

•Remain Truly Dynamic: Ordinary activity can further develop state of mind, diminish pressure, and improve in general prosperity.

•Keep a Fair Point of view: Keep difficulties in context, staying away from catastrophizing or limiting issues.

Building individual versatility is a continuous cycle, not an objective. It requires responsibility, persistence, and a readiness to get out of one's usual range of familiarity. By embracing misfortune, creating close to home spryness, cultivating mental strength, and sustaining an emotionally supportive network, people can outfit themselves with the devices important to flourish notwithstanding life's inescapable difficulties.

Chapter 3: Interpersonal Resilience: Strengthening Relationships

Relational flexibility is the ability to encourage, keep up with, and influence connections that add to our capacity to endure and recuperate from life's difficulties. This section dives into serious areas of strength for how, connections go about as a urgent emotionally supportive network, upgrading our flexibility by offering profound help, offering alternate points of view, and empowering development and transformation despite difficulty. We'll investigate systems for building tough connections and the significance of local area and association in our flexibility process.

The Significance of Social Help

Social help is a foundation of relational strength. It alludes to the mental and material assets given by an organization of caring people. These assets can fundamentally cushion against the impacts of pressure and affliction.

Sorts of Social Help:

•Everyday reassurance: Offering compassion, love, trust, and mindful.

•Educational Help: Sharing counsel, ideas, and data that assist people with adapting.

•Instrumental Help: Giving substantial guide and administrations that straightforwardly help an individual out of luck.

Advantages of Social Help:

•Improves confidence and self-assurance.

•Decreases tension and discouragement.

•Expands the capacity to adapt to pressure and recuperate from misfortune.

Conveying Actually

Powerful correspondence is essential in building and supporting tough connections. It includes communicating necessities, wants, and feelings in an unmistakable, legitimate, and conscious way, as well as effectively paying attention to other people.

Key Relational abilities:

•Undivided attention: Completely focusing, understanding, answering, and afterward recollecting what is being said.

•Sympathy: The capacity to comprehend and talk about the thoughts of another.

•Self-assuredness: Communicating one's own requirements and freedoms while regarding those of others.

Building Sympathy and Empathy

Sympathy and empathy are indispensable for cultivating profound, significant associations that help strength. These characteristics permit us to comprehend and connect with others' encounters, establishing a steady climate that supports sharing and common guide.

Developing Sympathy and Empathy:

•Practice undivided attention and be completely present in your collaborations.

•Envision yourself in the other individual's circumstance.

•Answer others' requirements with consideration and understanding.

Supporting Tough Connections

Strong connections are described by common regard, trust, and the capacity to usefully explore clashes. These connections support individual versatility as well as reinforce the strength of the actual relationship.

Procedures for Supporting Strong Connections:

•Ordinary Support: Put time and exertion into keeping up with connections through customary correspondence and shared encounters.

•Compromise: Move toward clashes as any open doors for development, looking for mutual benefit arrangements that regard every one of gatherings' necessities.

•Shared Values: Building connections on an underpinning of shared values and objectives can upgrade union and backing.

The Job of Local area

Past individual connections, being essential for a local area can enormously upgrade relational flexibility. Networks give a feeling of having a place, shared character, and aggregate help, which are all significant during seasons of emergency or difficulty.

Drawing in with Local area:

•Partake in neighborhood associations, clubs, or gatherings that line up with your inclinations or values.

•Volunteer for purposes you care about, which can likewise assist you with associating with similar people.

•Support others locally, perceiving that strength is many times an aggregate exertion.

Pragmatic Strides for Reinforcing Relational Versatility

•Cultivate Associations: Focus on it to assemble and keep up areas of strength for with.

•Be Proactive: Don't trust that an emergency will connect with others. Routinely draw in with your encouraging group of people.

•Practice Appreciation: Express appreciation for the help and cherish you get from others.

Relational flexibility isn't just about making due through difficulty; it's tied in with flourishing through the associations we cultivate with others. By building solid, sound connections and drawing in with our networks, we upgrade our own versatility as well as add to the strength of people around us.

Chapter 4: Professional Resilience: Thriving in the Workplace

Proficient versatility is the capacity to explore the intricacies, tensions, and difficulties of the work environment with certainty and flexibility. It's tied in with returning quickly from misfortunes, gaining from disappointment, and constantly looking for learning experiences. This section centers around techniques to construct strength in your vocation, upgrade work fulfillment, and accomplish proficient objectives, even notwithstanding difficulty.

Figuring out Proficient Difficulties

The cutting edge work environment can be a wellspring of huge pressure and difficulties, including position instability, high requests, tight cutoff times, and complex group elements. Perceiving and understanding these difficulties is the most vital move toward creating strength.

Normal Expert Difficulties:

•Change and Vulnerability: Quick mechanical headways, authoritative changes, and monetary variances can establish a climate of vulnerability.

•Responsibility and Tension: Elevated standards and requesting jobs can prompt pressure and burnout.

•Relational Struggles: Contrasts in characters, correspondence styles, and objectives can prompt contentions inside groups.

Adjusting to Change

In our current reality where change is the main steady, versatility is a critical part of expert flexibility. Adjusting to change includes remaining adaptable, mastering new abilities, and keeping an uplifting perspective toward new difficulties.

Procedures for Adjusting to Change:

•Remain Informed: Stay up with the latest with industry patterns, advances, and changes inside your association.

•Foster a Learning Outlook: View changes as any open doors to learn and develop expertly.

•Embrace Adaptability: Be available to better approaches for working, including acclimating to new group elements, innovations, or cycles.

Gaining from Disappointment

Disappointment is an inescapable piece of expert development. Strong experts view disappointments as significant opportunities for growth as opposed to unfavorable snags.

Moving toward Disappointment Helpfully:

•Dissect and Reflect: Carve out opportunity to examine what turned out badly and why. Ponder the illustrations gained from the experience.

•Look for Input: Productive criticism from friends, coaches, or bosses can give bits of knowledge and guide future endeavors.

•Keep up with Point of view: Comprehend that disappointment is a piece of the growing experience, not an impression of your value or capacities.

Building a Steady Organization

A solid expert organization can offer help, exhortation, and new open doors. It's a fundamental component of strength, offering an asset for coordinated effort, mentorship, and support.

Developing Proficient Connections:

•Organizing: Effectively participate in systems administration open doors inside and outside your association.

•Mentorship: Look for tutors who can give direction, guidance, and backing.

•Cooperation: Encourage cooperative associations with partners to share information and backing each other's development.

Overseeing Pressure and Keeping up with Prosperity

Viable pressure the board and taking care of oneself are critical for supporting proficient versatility. They empower people to keep up with their wellbeing, prosperity, and efficiency, considerably under tension.

Procedures for Overseeing Pressure:

•Focus on and Representative: Oversee responsibility actually by focusing on assignments and designating whenever the situation allows.

•Enjoy Reprieves: Customary breaks can help forestall burnout and keep up with center.

•Practice Taking care of oneself: Participate in exercises that advance physical, profound, and mental prosperity, like activity, leisure activities, and care rehearses.

Reasonable Strides for Improving Proficient Strength

•Put forth Reasonable Objectives: Spotlight on attainable expert objectives to inspire progress and assemble certainty.

•Foster Capacity to appreciate anyone on a profound level: Upgrade your capacity to deal with feelings and explore relational elements successfully.

•Look for Difficulties: Get out of your usual range of familiarity to handle new ventures or jobs that animate development and learning.

Proficient versatility isn't just about making due in the working environment; it's tied in with flourishing, accomplishing individual satisfaction, and contributing genuinely to your association. By embracing change, gaining from disappointment, building steady organizations, and overseeing pressure, people can explore their professions with strength, flexibility, and certainty.

Chapter 5: Cultural and Community Resilience

Social and local area versatility alludes to the limit of a gathering, society, or culture to endure and recuperate from misfortunes, like cataclysmic events, financial slumps, or social disturbances. This flexibility is established in the aggregate qualities, shared values, and informal organizations that tight spot networks together. This section digs into the systems that empower networks and societies to flourish in the midst of difficulties, featuring the significance of aggregate activity, shared liability, and common help.

Figuring out Aggregate Flexibility

Aggregate flexibility rises above individual survival techniques, including the common ability to answer and recuperate from emergencies. It includes the exchange of social, social, and financial elements that add to a local area's capacity to support and modify itself.

Components of Aggregate Strength:

•Shared Character and Values: major areas of strength for an of having a place and mutual perspective can prepare local area individuals towards shared objectives.

•Social Union: Trust, fortitude, and shared help inside a local area upgrade its ability to act all things considered in the midst of hardship.

•Versatile Limit: The capacity of a local area to adjust to evolving conditions, enhance arrangements, and gain from encounters.

The Job of Culture in Versatility

Culture assumes a basic part in molding reactions to misfortune. Social convictions, practices, and customs can give a system to understanding and overseeing emergencies, offering solace and a feeling of congruity.

Social Strength Components:

•Narrating and Accounts: Sharing accounts of endurance and recuperation can move trust and give models to strength.

•Social Practices: Customs, functions, and local meetings can fortify bonds and backing close to home mending.

•Social Qualities: Values like correspondence, philanthropy, and local area administration can inspire aggregate activity and backing.

Building Tough People group

Creating people group flexibility is a proactive cycle that includes reinforcing the social texture and improving the local area's ability to all in all face difficulties.

Systems for Building People group Strength:

•Local area Commitment: Empowering dynamic support in local area life and dynamic cycles fortifies local area bonds.

•Limit Building: Putting resources into schooling, framework, and nearby economies upgrades a local area's capacity to endure shocks.

•Joint effort and Associations: Organizations between local area associations, government offices, and organizations can pool assets and mastery to address normal difficulties.

Instances of Versatile People group

From the beginning of time, there have been various instances of networks that have shown wonderful flexibility notwithstanding misfortune. These models give significant illustrations on the force of aggregate activity and the significance of local area readiness.

•Recuperation from Cataclysmic events: Networks that have effectively remade after cataclysmic events, frequently through grassroots getting sorted out and utilizing nearby information.

•Financial Renewal: Regions that have gone through monetary change by encouraging advancement, business, and local area drove improvement.

•Social Attachment In the midst of Emergency: Social orders that experience kept up with social union and harmony notwithstanding struggle or cultural changes, through discourse, compromise, and comprehensive arrangements.

Viable Strides for Improving Social and Local area Versatility

•Cultivate People group Organizations: Make and keep up with networks that can assemble assets and backing in the midst of emergency.

•Observe Social Legacy: Safeguard and advance social practices that add to a feeling of personality and having a place.

•Plan for What's in store: Take part in local area arranging and readiness exercises to alleviate the effects of likely emergencies.

Social and local area flexibility is tied in with tackling the aggregate strength and shrewdness of a gathering to explore the difficulties of a steadily impacting world. It highlights the significance of fortitude, shared liability, and dynamic commitment to cultivating conditions where networks can get by as well as flourish.

Chapter 6: Tools and Techniques for Developing Resilience

This section presents an assortment of useful instruments and strategies intended to fortify versatility at an individual and local area level. Creating flexibility is a continuous cycle, and integrating these systems into day to day existence can help construct the psychological, close to home, and social determination expected to confront life's difficulties. From care practices to versatility preparing programs, these methodologies offer pathways to a stronger presence.

Care and Contemplation

Care and contemplation have been displayed to influence emotional wellness and strength fundamentally. By advancing consciousness of the current second and encouraging a non-critical mentality, these practices can assist with diminishing pressure, upgrade close to home guideline, and work on mental adaptability.

Key Practices:

•Care Reflection: Normal act of care contemplation can upgrade center and diminish rumination around regrettable considerations.

•Breathing Activities: Basic breathing procedures can assist with quieting the psyche and body, diminishing pressure and uneasiness.

•Body Outputs: This training includes focusing on different pieces of the body and seeing any sensations, pressures, or inconvenience, which advances substantial mindfulness and unwinding.

Mental Conduct Methodologies

Mental conduct methodologies center around recognizing and testing negative idea examples and convictions, advancing more adjusted and valuable reasoning.

Methods Include:

•Mental Rebuilding: Recognizing negative, pointless considerations and supplanting them with additional positive and sensible ones.

•Critical thinking Preparing: Creating abilities to successfully handle issues, decreasing the inclination to feel overpowered by difficulties.

•Objective Setting: Setting clear, feasible objectives coordinates concentration and encourages a feeling of achievement and reason.

Building The ability to appreciate anyone on a deeper level

Creating the ability to appreciate anyone on a deeper level includes working on mindfulness, feeling guideline, sympathy, and interactive abilities, which are critical for strength.

Ways Of improving Capacity to appreciate individuals on a profound level:

•Journaling: Pondering individual encounters and feelings through journaling can increment mindfulness and understanding.

•Criticism Chasing: Helpful input from others can give experiences into one's close to home reactions and relational abilities.

•Sympathy Activities: Working on seeing circumstances according to others' points of view can upgrade compassion and work on friendly associations.

Actual Wellbeing

Actual wellbeing assumes a huge part in building flexibility, as a solid body upholds areas of strength for a.

Key Components:

•Standard Activity: Actual work isn't just valuable for actual wellbeing yet in addition further develops state of mind and lessens tension.

•Nourishment: A reasonable eating regimen can influence emotional well-being and energy levels, supporting by and large strength.

•Rest Cleanliness: Satisfactory rest is fundamental for mental capability, profound guideline, and actual wellbeing.

Local area and Social Help

Constructing and keeping up major areas of strength for with associations are fundamental for flexibility. Networks and organizations offer help, assets, and a feeling of having a place.

Procedures for Reinforcing Associations:

•Local area Contribution: Taking part in local area occasions, gatherings, or chip in open doors can construct a steady organization.

•Interactive abilities Preparing: Further developing correspondence and relational abilities can improve connections and emotionally supportive networks.

•Support Gatherings: Joining bunches for individuals with comparative difficulties or objectives can offer profound help and important exhortation.

Coordinating Strength Practices

Integrating these devices and procedures into everyday schedules can make enduring changes in how people and networks answer pressure and difficulty. About picking systems resound actually and focusing on ordinary practice.

•Begin Little: Start with a couple of practices and bit by bit integrate more as they become ongoing.

•Be Steady: Standard practice is vital to building flexibility. Put away unambiguous times every day for strength building exercises.

•Look for Help: Drawing in with companions, family, or local area individuals on the strength building excursion can give inspiration and responsibility.

Creating versatility is a dynamic and individual excursion. By utilizing these apparatuses and methods, people and networks can develop the strength and adaptability expected to explore life's difficulties with beauty and arise more grounded and more associated.

Chapter 7: Looking Ahead: The Future of Resilience

As we explore a consistently impacting world, the idea of strength turns out to be progressively essential. This last part investigates the fate of strength, taking into account arising difficulties and the potential for versatility to drive development, development, and positive change in people, networks, and social orders. We'll inspect the patterns forming the future scene and how developing flexibility can set us up to figure out these difficulties.

Arising Difficulties

What's to come presents a progression of remarkable difficulties that will test our flexibility on various fronts. From environmental change and natural debasement to mechanical headways and the moving elements of work and society, these difficulties require versatile reactions and imaginative arrangements.

Key Difficulties Include:

•Natural Changes: Environmental change presents critical dangers to worldwide wellbeing, security, and assets, requiring versatile reactions from networks and countries.

•Mechanical Disturbance: Advances in simulated intelligence, advanced mechanics, and computerized innovations are changing businesses, work markets, and cultural designs, requiring people and associations to quickly adjust.

•Social and Monetary Movements: Globalization, segment changes, and financial unpredictability present complex difficulties for social attachment and financial security.

Strength as an Impetus for Development

Even with these difficulties, versatility arises as a guarded system as well as a proactive instrument for development and development. By embracing versatility, adaptability, and a ground breaking outlook, strength can drive clever fixes to complex issues.

Creative Ways to deal with Versatility:

•Manageable Turn of events: Utilizing versatility remembering to make reasonable, versatile frameworks that safeguard the climate while advancing monetary and social prosperity.

•Mechanical Advancement: Creating versatile innovations that can adjust to changing circumstances and backing human prosperity notwithstanding computerization and advanced change.

•Social Advancement: Developing versatile networks that can explore social and monetary movements, encouraging inclusivity, variety, and value.

Building Versatility for What's in store

Planning for what's to come requires a deliberate work to reinforce strength at all degrees of society. This includes individual and local area versatility building endeavors as well as foundational changes that improve the flexibility and supportability of our worldwide frameworks.

Systems for Future Flexibility:

•Training and Long lasting Getting the hang of: Advancing strength through instruction that stresses decisive reasoning, flexibility, and the capacity to understand people on a profound level, planning people for a quickly influencing world.

•Strategy and Administration: Executing arrangements that cultivate monetary, ecological, and social strength, guaranteeing that frameworks are strong, versatile, and impartial.

•Local area and Worldwide Joint effort: Empowering cooperation across networks, countries, and areas to address worldwide difficulties with aggregate insight and shared assets.

The Job of Every Person in Forming What's to come

The fate of flexibility isn't foreordained; it is molded by the activities and choices of every person. By developing individual flexibility, we add to a stronger society fit for confronting future difficulties with strength and confidence. A significant investment of time and energy to construct strength, regardless of how little, is a stage towards a more versatile, creative, and economical future.

•Embrace Change: View change as a chance for development and getting the hang of, remaining open to new encounters and thoughts.

•Encourage People group: Fortify social associations and local area ties, perceiving the force of aggregate activity and backing.

•Act with Reason: Adjust activities to individual qualities and objectives, contributing emphatically to the more extensive cultural and natural setting.

As we look forward, obviously strength will be a vital determinant of progress and prosperity in the 21st 100 years. By embracing the standards and practices of flexibility framed in this book, we can explore the vulnerabilities representing things to come with certainty, transforming difficulties into open doors for development, development, and positive change.

www.ingramcontent.com/pod-product-compliance
Lightning Source LLC
Chambersburg PA
CBHW030509170726
47990CB00008BA/3117